T0196345

God Spoke
To
Me

Coach Roscoe

authorHOUSE®

AuthorHouse™
1663 Liberty Drive
Bloomington, IN 47403
www.authorhouse.com
Phone: 1 (800) 839-8640

Published by AuthorHouse 06/26/2017

ISBN: 978-1-5246-9734-1 (sc)
ISBN: 978-1-5246-9733-4 (e)

Library of Congress Control Number: 2017909682

Print information available on the last page.

*Any people depicted in stock imagery provided by Thinkstock are models,
and such images are being used for illustrative purposes only.
Certain stock imagery © Thinkstock.*

This book is printed on acid-free paper.

Scripture taken from the King James Version of the Bible.

God Spoke
To
Me

I would like to say thank you to Asia Blaney for seeing this book opportunity before I did and for her encouragement and support while writing this book.

Romans 12:2 And be not conformed to this world but be ye transformed by the renewing of your mind that ye may prove what is that good and acceptable and perfect will of God

CONTENTS

STRUGGLE

Struggle – What is struggle?

It's not being broke.

Struggle is not trying to just survive in the world paying bills.

Struggle is spiritual.

For some when you have not one person to talk to.

Struggle is when you know you coming against demons and think you're losing a spiritual fight.

You're getting attack after attack and think you can't pray.

That's struggle.

When you struggle to find a way to pray.

Struggle is hard.

When you know what's right, you see what's right, but you feel alone.

But you got God there sitting back waiting on you to call Him.

He's not going to call you in your struggle.

You will come out of your struggle if you get right and just talk to God.

He will help you.

Struggle is not just gonna go away the next day.

Stay on the path to get to be the God-fearing person you're supposed to be.

Struggle is when you have someone in your face, but you keep cool because that's God's way.

Struggle will never go away especially if you trying to walk with God.

But think Jesus struggled a long time so stay strong in prayer.

Don't do what you used to do and try to not do anything you know God won't like

And really

You never know when you come across an angel (and yes they're real).

So struggle can make you stronger spiritually.

But struggle is to not turn back to what you used to be.

It's what you are walking into to be great!

REFLECTION

FAMILY

Family is not just people with the same blood you have or not even wife and kids, but family is people you miss and people that miss you and need you.

Not for money

But they might need your smile

Or just your hello.

Don't think because you're not here you're not thought of,

just because you don't get a call you're not loved.

So stay strong because you never know who misses you or even considers you as family.

Truthfully we're all supposed to be family because we are all God's children.

You're supposed to consider everyone brother or sister.

We are all God's children and church is our home.

So always come home and stay close to your family, your church family also.

REFLECTION

TO SHAKE
A DEMON

When you know God has a calling on you, demons come strong and fast on you.

But you have to learn how to shake them demons.

Not just going to church Tuesdays and Sundays are you going to shake them demons.

No! You must stay prayerful.

Not just before you go to bed but stay in a prayerful mind, set all day, every day.

That is still not the only way you shake a demon.

You must wear blessed oil from the man of God.

What we have to do to shake a demon is to call on the Name of Jesus in time of your hard moments.

No money, call "Jesus"

No car, call "Jesus".

Those demons want you to think you won't make it.

Demons play mind games to make you feel lonely, depressed, broke.

But God says different!

Shake them demons off smoking.

Pray, call on Jesus.

Shake them demons off.

Depression

Call on Jesus, shake them demons off.

Drinking

Call the Name of Jesus, shake them demons off.

Anger

Call Jesus to help you, stay humble. Shake them demons off.

You call the Name of Jesus and stay prayerful.

Feed your soul with the Bible every day, gospel music.

Them demons will run but don't think they won't be upset.

Oh, they will but call the Name of Jesus.

Them demons going to be mad but

Remember you must keep your mind on things that will please God

Every day not just some days

That's how you shake them demons.

Keep a Bible in your pocket and you shake demons.

Read the Word, play gospel music every day, pray all day.

Stay happy even when you think you can't be happy.

You will shake demons.

But remember to shake a demon you better know you will shake demons every day.

It's like playing basketball. If you're a guard, you have to shake the defense. Just like if you are a running back, you have to shake that linebacker.

Shake them demons off you!

The devil didn't want me to write this, but I shook my pen and said God's Name and it worked to shake a demon and I started writing so I could shake some demons off.

Them demons can't keep a hold on you unless you do the opposite of what God says.

Demons can't keep a hold of you.

Shake them demons off you.

Them demons will make you feel heavy like not fat but like weights holding you down.

Shake them demons off you and see how lifht you feel.

Them demons will even make you think life is over.

But shake them demons and live for God.

REFLECTION

THE STORY OF
A MAN OF GOD

A man of God is a man that walks in faith even though he was told you won't live past 16 or 21.

A man of God walks in faith when you have something like a bone infection you're supposed to die from, but you live and it goes away.

A man of God repents for his past. Just because you drank liquor, doesn't mean you're not a man of God.

Just because you've been involved in street activity, doesn't mean you're not a man of God.

You might have had to see something and be involved in things to know its wrong and not of God and to find out a man of God is not of this world, He's just in it.

A man of God might go through things that the average man can't handle, but that man of God knows how to talk to God and trust God will bring him through.

Like Pastor Shelby said to me, "You have a target on your chest so you're going to get attacks, but you have to trust in God."

Like Elder Clifton said before, "You will be lied on, talked about. Your family might not talk to you. Your friends might turn their back on you. But, you're still a man of God. You might be dragged in the mud. But, you're still a man of God."

Just because he didn't show he was a man of God, he knew but was running.

You have to remember, he's human, he's made mistakes in the past, but they made him stronger in God and mentally.

It was and is a process. Nobody's perfect like Pastor Shelby said once. If we were perfect we would be in heaven, but none of us are in heaven. So don't judge a man of God by his past, judge him if you must on how he conducts himself in the now as Pastor Shelby says in the now.

But truthfully you shouldn't judge anyone. You're not God and as Pastor Shelby said before we're not living by a law, an old law, so don't judge a man of God.

It's not easy to do things to only please God, but you are a man of God.

Just because you had to lose everything you had doesn't mean you're not a man of God.

If you remember Pastor Shelby said you might have to lose your house and some things, but you're a man of God.

It might help you write your sermon, so don't judge a man of God because he had to struggle to get to where he's at now.

A MAN OF GOD!

REFLECTION

The enemy made me feel like he's bigger and stronger, but I had to swing back, keeping my Bible in my pocket.

But the enemy threw sin after sin in my face.

But I had to ask God to help me hit back

Listening to the gospel,

Asking for mercy.

The enemy pressed down on me harder.

Swing back with a praise to God

Swing back. Read your Bible

Swing back. Play gospel music at work.

Swing back. Speak of God.

Swing back. Be humble.

Swing back. Play gospel music and read the Bible at the same time and knock the enemy out and prove he's not bigger and stronger than God.

REFLECTION

SEEK AND DESTROY

REFLECTION

NO BLOOD ON MY HANDS

I got tired of mixed up feelings that were coming every day.

And they weren't just built up any more, they were coming out

Anger, sadness, lonely, not wanting to be here, trying to hide from the world.

I was not listening to God but he forced me to hear because He spoke to me, through me. I thought I was going crazy, but it was a lot of power in the voice, a lot!

"You want things to ease up? Come to Me. Give Me what I want."

"What's that God?"

"You give Me, you. Become the man of God I spared your life to be and things will ease up around you. If not, you will have blood on your hands. Don't play with Me. I'm nothing to play with. You will become a minister. You will hear my voice as you have. You will work for Me and only Me. You will not do sins you used to do."

So I asked God to clean me, deliver me. I put everything in God's hands.

I will minister. I will obey.

What you don't understand is I have no choice. I don't want blood on my hands.

Because it's people out there that might not know God, and I might be the only person they're listening to, to find God.

So for God sparing me several times, I will do God's work and no blood will be on my hands.

REFLECTION

STRIPPED

Thanksgiving and Christmas I was alone, stripped of a car and the real food of the holidays.

That was God's way of saying, "Can you survive without Me?"

"Barely. I was put in the middle of sin, prostitutes, dope addicts and liquor store around me. Basically this is God saying to me, "Choose."

Instead of getting liquor, I read the Bible.

Instead of thinking of a woman, I read the Bible.

Instead of turning to a drug, I read my Bible.

Some very lonely days, I read my Bible.

I am not embarrassed to tell you, I have been stripped because I had money and partied and stuff and friends.

But even though I had all worldly choices, I chose God's way so I don't mind that I was stripped.

REFLECTION

I WON'T COMPLAIN

Even though it's a song, it was real life for me.

I struggled.

I was stripped of all worldly things and was dead smack in the middle of sin.

But I don't complain.

I grew up with a disability, grew up not knowing when it's my last day alive.

But I didn't complain.

I grew up struggling spiritually.

But I didn't complain.

Like first lady said on morning cup one day, "The tree and grass are green and you're breathing fresh air and the sun shines and it rains."

I had some good days.
I had a lot of hills to climb in my life.
I had many weary days and lonely nights.
AND
Just when I think things over,
All my God-given good days outweigh my bad days.
I won't complain!

It's times when my clouds hang low.
But the question!

Lord,
Why so much pain?
Why so much struggle?
Why so much junk?

But He knows what's best for me and what I can handle even though my weary eyes just don't see in the midst of adversity.

I just only know to say, "Thank you, Lord, I won't complain." But believe me when I tell you God has been good to me more than the world will ever be.

God has been good to me the days that I cried in my life.
He dried my tears away.

Turned my midnights into day so I will just say, "Thank you, Lord," because He's been good to me.

I'm still alive after it being said I won't live past 15 or 16.
And 21 then had a bone infection.

God's been good to me and I know I haven't been the best or done everything I should have in my life.
But I still say, "Thank you, Lord."

Been lied on, persecuted and called everything but a man of God.
But, "Thank you, Lord."
I won't,
You ain't going to make me,
I can't,
I won't complain.

REFLECTION

ANOINTED

Anointing is nothing to play with.

Some people play with it like they can be holy only on Sunday and Bible study nights.

But God is not sometimes.

He's all the time.

There is no giving it back.

No turning back.

You are anointed and you better do as God says and do His will.

Because if not you are in more danger then the next man is.

Just because you didn't start off doing all the right things, don't mean you not anointed.

Some people weren't taught on how to walk into their anointing.

But remember you had to learn your gifts or your anointing.

So don't judge, only God can judge.

But when you learn or realize there is no turning back, you better do as God says to do.

Because God is nothing to play with.

And remember you may be anointed so walk in it.

REFLECTION

SOME PAIN

Some pain is connected to the enemy.

Hangovers from drinking,

When your head hurts that's the enemy, not God.

When you're burning from a STD.

That's one reason you should wait to have sex when you're married.

Pain can also be a result of something that the enemy tricked you to do.

Breaking in someone's house, you can get shot, be put in the hospital or even die.

This is pain, hangovers, STDs, gunshot wounds from you robbing is all pain connected to the enemy.

But don't think that's the only pain you get.

You can be a person with many women.

Pain can be connected to this also because of some point in your life the same way you hurt women, you will receive some kind of pain from a woman such as her cheating, taking your money or just flat out harming you like stabbing or shooting you.

So don't think by having a few women at the same time you won't get hurt.

So it's best to do the thing that pleases God because God won't hurt you.

God won't give you a headache for soaking up His word instead of soaking up that liquor.

God won't make your genitals burn.

But God will put you on fire for Him.

REFLECTION

Printed in the United States
By Bookmasters